The World of
GUINNESS

Rory Guinness

SCALA

'Guinness's Dublin Stout. This article is confidently recommended for home consumption and for export, and must, from its age, purity and soundness, ensure the approbation and support of the Public'.

The Morning Post, 1829

Ingredients

Foreword

PEOPLE OFTEN ASK what it means to be a Guinness. The first word that comes to mind is pride.

If you have a surname such as Guinness, it is hard to escape from it. I still marvel at what it means in different countries around the world.

Over the years, my family has taken credit for achievements that in fact couldn't have taken place without the support of a much wider team. When my family was actively running the brewery, we developed a nose for selecting exceptionally talented individuals, known traditionally as 'Guinness People'.

It is wonderful to know that this tradition of talent lives on in the form of Paul Carty, Eibhlin Roche and their colleagues at the Guinness Storehouse, to whom I am deeply indebted.

To some, St James's Gate Brewery may seem an old, even unsightly industrial site. To me it is a home. It is where two generations of my family lived. It is where my father Benjamin Iveagh, the last family chairman of Guinness, went to work for thirty years. And it is where my wife Mira agreed to marry me. It is the centre of the world of Guinness.

It is almost impossible to condense the world of Guinness into one small book, but welcome anyway to its many parts.

RORY GUINNESS

A Great Dublin Venture

BREWERS HAVE BEEN STRIVING to create a faultless brew for thousands of years. The ancient Egyptians were the first to try, but it was not until 1759 that Arthur Guinness began the process that culminated in the perfect pint.

When Arthur Guinness (1725–1803) left behind his family's small brewery in Leixlip, Co. Kildare, to seek his fortunes in Dublin, many must have thought he was mad. The brewing business in Dublin was in a terrible way, with excise laws favouring imported beers. With just £100 in his pocket, money that he had inherited from his previous employer, Dr Arthur Price, Archbishop of Cashel, he went about setting up his brewery. Fortunately, Arthur had an eye for a bargain. Even though the ill-equipped brewery at St James's Gate had been disused for many years, he could see that acquiring the property for an annual rent of £45 was a good deal. The lease, which was for 9,000 years, was signed in 1759. A copy of it is preserved in the floor of the atrium of Guinness Storehouse.

Arthur was attracted to St James's Gate because of its size

Portrait of Arthur Guinness, founder (1725–1803)

Early 19th–century illustration of St James's Gate Brewery

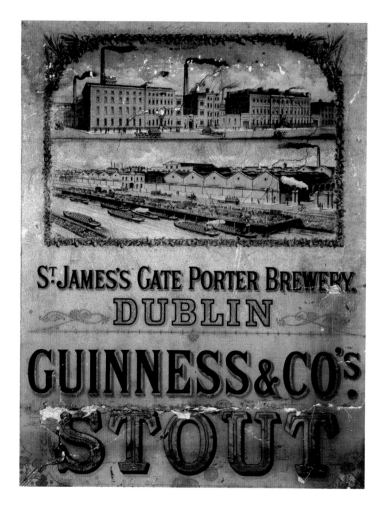

Advertising showcard featuring illustration of St James's Gate Porter Brewery, Dublin, c.1890

and unique location close to the centre of Dublin. He saw that the site had many benefits. With the pure water sourced from the Rivers Dodder and Poddle, and the proximity of the canals for transport, he could import the finest raw ingredients and export the finest beers. When he arrived at the four-acre site, Arthur faced intense rivalry from more than seventy breweries operating in Dublin at the time. For these competitors, quality was not a main concern; for Arthur, it was of the greatest importance. His site consisted of only a copper (a giant kettle), a kieve (a Dublin term for a mash tun which acts like a giant sieve), a mill, two malt houses, stables for twelve horses and a loft that could hold 200 tons of hay. Despite the simplicity of his brewery, Arthur was able to begin

Fanlight of 1 Thomas Street, home of Arthur Guinness

producing some of the finest brew Dublin had ever seen.

In 1761, Arthur married the Dublin heiress Olivia Whitmore. They went on to have twenty-one children. When not attending to his very busy family and public life, Arthur Guinness was brewing mostly the ales and light beers which were so popular at the time. However, he soon noticed a new trend. Arthur had seen a dark beer being drunk with increasing popularity by the porters of Covent Garden market and Billingsgate market in London. As a result, he began brewing his own porter. Within a matter of years, Arthur's experiment had become so successful that after his death in 1803, his son Arthur II (1768–1855) devoted more and more resources to this new, dark brew. Soon, foreign buyers began to arrive in Dublin unsolicited to buy Guinness porter. Word was spreading that Dublin was brewing something special.

First trademark label issued by Guinness in 1862 showing the HARP symbol, trademarked in 1876 and based on the Brian Boru harp preserved in Trinity College

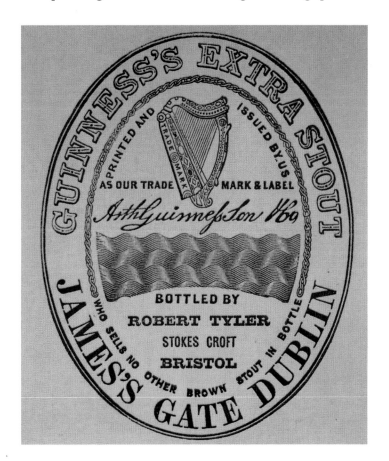

Guinness Storehouse

Interior view of Market
Street Storehouse, St
James's Gate Brewery,
featuring a view into the
building through one of the
four lightwells, c.1906–10

View of Market Street
Storehouse taken from the
south-east corner at the
south end of St James's
Gate Brewery, c.1906–10

Overleaf: Workers crossing
the Brewery yard at St
James's Gate Brewery,
c.1906

THE RAPID GROWTH IN DEMAND for Guinness beer throughout the 1800s meant that more space was needed in order to increase production. As the company went from strength to strength, it began to expand the St James's Gate site, buying surrounding land and buildings. The booming business needed more space so that it could remain focused on improving brewing techniques. It did this in the manner in which it knew best – by employing only the finest and most modern resources to ensure optimum quality.

A new fermentation plant (the building where the fourth ingredient, yeast, is added to the brew) was needed. This led to the construction of Market Street Storehouse, the first multi-storey building in the British Isles to be built with a steel frame. The Storehouse was completed in 1904, just before the

other notable steel-framed building of its time, the Ritz Hotel in London. The Storehouse, whose design is attributed to the chief brewery engineer, A. H. Hignett, was constructed at an incredible pace, and all work was completed in just over a year.

There was undoubtedly an American influence to its design – of the Chicago School. The widely spaced steel frame and stanchions were sited to allow more light to penetrate the building. The Storehouse is almost square, with its steel structure exposed on the interior but encased in brick on the exterior. Sir William Arrol and Co. of Glasgow designed the intricate steelwork. When the building was opened, a national newspaper stated that 'Irish firms are capable of emulating and, in this case, excelling the achievements of contemporaries across the Channel and in America, both as regards workmanship and rapidity of execution.'

The Storehouse quickly emerged as a crucial part of the

A. H. Hignett, Engineer-in-Chief at St James's Gate Brewery, 1902–29

Opposite: Skimming off
excess yeast, Market Street
Storehouse, c.1906

Below: View through pint-
shaped glass atrium of
Guinness Storehouse

Bottom: Exterior view of
Guinness Storehouse

Oriel windows on the east side of the Guinness Storehouse building

Gravity Bar 'hovering' over the top of the Guinness Storehouse building

Gravity Bar,
Guinness Storehouse

Opposite: Nocturnal
view of Guinness
Storehouse

brewery infrastructure. It was used to accommodate the new sixteen-tun fermentation plant, and the first fermentation took place there on Friday 2 March 1906. The plant could produce an extraordinary 65,000,000 gallons (295,500,000 litres) of Guinness beer every year. The Storehouse was used as a fermentation plant until 1986, when a new state-of-the-art plant was built elsewhere on the brewery site. In 1997, the company Diageo began transforming the Storehouse into an amazing tribute to Guinness's past and its future. The fascinating story it tells is of a family of brewers and how they managed to globalise their unique brew.

Interior view of the Brewers'
Sampling Room, 1948

'We are Brewers and always have been;
and in our brewing we have sought,
and we seek, to ally the traditions and
craftsmanship of the past with the best
that science has to teach us.'

Rupert Guinness, Chairman, 1949

The Brewing Process

ONLY THE FINEST INGREDIENTS are used in the production of Guinness beer, and it is thanks to these high standards that you get such a fine pint.

Preparation is key, and the Guinness brewers use the very best barley, water, hops and yeast. They take a centuries-old technique and apply it with all the benefits of modern brewing. No artificial preservatives or additives of any kind are used.

Before the brewing process can begin, the raw ingredients need to be sourced and prepared. St James's Gate gathers its barley from all over Ireland. The barley is converted to malt off-site by steeping it in water under minutely controlled conditions. These grains are then ready to release the sugars needed for fermentation.

Some additional barley is roasted but certainly not burnt (contrary to popular belief) in the Roast House. The roasted barley gives the pint its wonderful, distinctive ruby red colour and taste. The finest hops are sourced from all over the world

View of the top of the malt bins in Robert Street Malt Store, 1948

Interior view of Cooke's Lane Maltings, St James's Gate Brewery, 1948

Three labourers clearing out spent hops from a Hop-back in the Brewhouse, St James's Gate Brewery, 1948

Interior view of a vat house, St James's Gate Brewery, 1948

Shaping a wooden cask, Cooperage Workshop, St James's Gate Brewery, 1948

View across the Racking Shed, St James's Gate Brewery, c.1906–10

Interior view of kieve stage in the Brewhouse, St James's Gate Brewery, c.1906–10

Kettles in the Brewhouse, St James's Gate Brewery, c.1994

The end product – the perfect pint

to give Guinness its unique bitterness and aroma, as well as acting as a natural preservative.

Water is sourced from the fresh springs and reservoirs of the Wicklow Mountains, which border Dublin. The key elements are its softness and purity, which provide the base for a perfect pint. Liffey water has never been used in the production of Guinness.

The yeast is the key to bonding all of these elements together. It transforms the nutrients and natural sugars from the brewing process into Guinness.

The brewing process proper starts in the Brewhouse. The malted and roasted barley is mixed and milled together to produce the coarse Guinness grist. The grist then heads to the mash vessel, where it is mixed with water heated to 65°C. This is the perfect temperature for optimal enzyme activity, enabling the starches contained in the barley to be converted into sugars.

When the milling and mashing are completed, the mash is transferred to a kieve, which acts as a giant sieve. This removes all the unwanted solids and lets the sugary liquid – known as 'wort' – filter through to the giant kettle. In the kettle, the hops are added and the contents are boiled for ninety minutes. The sterile brew is then left to settle and cool before being aerated.

The final stage is fermentation, when yeast is added to the brew. It is carefully blended and repeatedly tested to make sure that each brew reaches the same high quality.

Now the full, delicious flavour of Guinness has evolved, together with the natural carbon dioxide, which is an essential part of the famous creamy head.

Loading wooden casks onto lorries for delivery, St James's Gate Brewery, 1948

Lorries pulling out of the Loading Bank laden with wooden casks, St James's Gate Brewery, 1948

Guinness on the Move

ONE OF ARTHUR GUINNESS'S GREATEST TRIUMPHS was finding such a well-placed property. The brewery once formed part of the outer wall of the City of Dublin, next to the gate of St James, which was one of the principal entrances for trade coming from the countryside to the west of Dublin. Arthur was attracted to the site for the quality of its water, and also for the

Barge laden with wooden casks on the River Liffey, 1948

quality of its water links. It is very conveniently situated near the Grand Canal, as well as the River Liffey, and latterly one of Ireland's main railway stations, Heuston Station.

In the early days, Arthur had to rely on the horse and cart to transport his products around Dublin. At this time, the market for his Guinness ales and stout was limited to Dublin. However, the whole system of transportation was about to change.

The brewery was linked to the Grand Canal through St James's Street Harbour. Boats carrying the best raw materials could be brought to the brewery from the country, and were able to return to the country laden with barrels of Guinness beer.

With the twenty-five-fold expansion of the brewery over its first 150 years, internal transportation became a major issue.

Guinness barge, the *Clonsilla*, sailing west up the River Liffey underneath the Ha'penny Bridge, *c.*1955

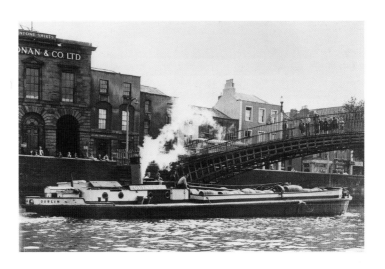

In response to this new challenge, the brewery developed its own rail system. The different levels of the brewery, from Victoria Quay at sea level to the high point at the Storehouse some sixty feet above, are all connected by a narrow-gauge railway, which at its peak covered some eight miles. Small locomotives were used to convey raw materials around the site. The ascent from the middle to the upper level is made through a special tunnel constructed using the corkscrew principle. The gradient in the brewery is one in thirty-nine, with a rise of twenty-five feet. The internal railway also linked up with the national rail network at Heuston Station to distribute Guinness around the country.

From 1873 to 1961, the company employed steam and later mechanised barges to carry the barrels along the River Liffey to Dublin Docks. The barrels were often destined for

Cleansing Shed, St James's Gate Brewery, c.1906

exotic lands. Local children would frequently crowd over the bridges as the barges went under, and shout to the crew, 'Bring us back a parrot, Mister!'

An important new era in Irish maritime history commenced in 1913 with the launching of the *WM Barkley*, the first of the company's own fleet of ships, which were to carry the product to foreign parts. The last Guinness ship was launched in 1976, the *Miranda Guinness*, which was the world's first ever beer-tanker vessel. (Incidentally, she was the last ship to be launched from the Bristol docks.) She was used extensively on the routes to Manchester and Liverpool to carry Guinness from Dublin to the markets of the north of England, Scotland and beyond. The majority of the Guinness ships were named after women of the Guinness family. My mother, Miranda Guinness, still does not like being called a bulk liquid carrier!

SS Guinness in Dublin port, 1948

Straker Squire steam
lorries, St James's Gate
Brewery, c.1900

Thornycroft steam lorry,
St James's Gate Brewery,
c.1900

Guinness truck with barrels
in front of the Customs
House, c.1950

Fleet of Guinness Vulcan
lorries laden for town
deliveries awaits dispatch at
Victoria Quay, c.1956

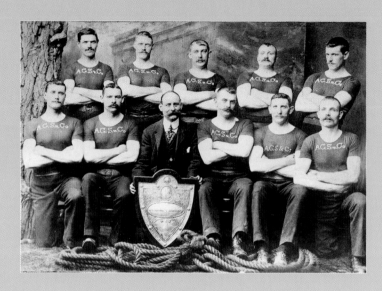

St James's Gate Brewery
Tug-o-War team, 1904–05

Brewery families riding the
carousel at the Queen's
Day Fete in the Royal
Dublin Society Ground,
Ballsbridge, Dublin, c.1904

Brewery Life

THE BREWERY HAS BEEN at the cutting edge of brewing science throughout its history, but its real secret weapon is its people. It has always done its very best to look after them. My great grandfather, Rupert Iveagh, in his Chairman's speech to shareholders at the Annual General Meeting of 1949, said that Company Directors have 'always felt that it was not only the duty, but to the advantage, of the company and the shareholders, that the company should bear its part in serving this civilisation and the way of life in which we all believe.'

Guinness always offered better pay than other companies, as well as incredible job security. Records exist of non-contributory pensions being provided to employees as early as 1860. Should a husband or wife die, special care would be taken of the surviving family through the provision of jobs, a

Interior view of the Tap Room, with a line of men partaking of their allowance from metal tankards, 1948

Brewery employees in
the Dining Hall in the
Belview Workmen's
Rooms, St James's Gate
Brewery, c.1940–45

widow's allowance and even meals. By 1930, the brewery had
just over 5,000 people on its books (including those receiving
a pension), in addition to almost 9,000 more who were
employed indirectly. This amounted to nearly one in ten Dublin
men being maintained directly or indirectly by payments from
the brewery. Employees, pensioners and their families could
also take advantage of free health care at home or in hospital.
The company doctor was a regular part of family life for
Guinness employees, long before the Irish State organised

Pharmaceutical chemists at
work in the pharmacy at the
Dispensary, St James's
Gate Brewery, c.1940–45

Children taking part in a race during a Queen's Day Fete at the Royal Dublin Society Ground, Ballsbridge, Dublin, c.1902

such care. Brewery Mutual Societies were established to help employees with cheap loans for the purchase of homes, and career advancement through the ranks was encouraged with free education and prizes.

Female members of the Guinness catering staff enjoying bottles of Guinness, c.1957

One benefit of working in a brewery was the provision of two free pints a day to every male employee over 21 years. If you didn't drink, you could receive vouchers instead.

Brewery children gathered
inside Iveagh Play Centre,
enjoying their daily cup of
cocoa and a sticky bun,
*c.*1954

Public Life

WHEN ARTHUR II RETIRED in 1855, after having increased output by 10% per annum with the introduction of his new stronger brew, Guinness Extra Superior Porter, the brewery passed down to his son, Benjamin Lee Guinness. Like his father and grandfather before him, Benjamin Lee cared deeply for the welfare of his fellow Dubliners.

Benjamin Lee Guinness was devoted to public life, becoming Lord Mayor of Dublin in 1851, as well as the local member for parliament. He dedicated an enormous amount of personal and financial resources to the restoration of St Patrick's Cathedral and the rebuilding of The Coombe Women's Hospital. Marshes Library also fell within his benefaction. A year before his death in 1868, Benjamin Lee was ennobled for his works in business and in public life.

Benjamin Lee left the brewery to his two sons. They must have had an incredible childhood, living with their parents on St Stephen's Green in the building that is now Iveagh House,

Iveagh Play Centre with St Patrick's Park in the foreground, c.1940

where the Department of Foreign Affairs is housed. Working as private secretaries, they learnt the ropes of the business under the tutelage of their father. Edward Cecil Guinness undertook a part-time degree at Trinity College but never benefited from a full-time university career. Nevertheless, he went on to become Chancellor of the University.

In 1876, Arthur Guinness, the elder of Benjamin Lee Guinness's two sons, began an inspiring programme of philanthropy. Ably assisted by his wife Olive, one of his achievements was to remodel St Stephen's Green, and today he sits on a plinth in the park that he helped to create, opposite the Royal College of Surgeons. Edward Cecil Guinness, later 1st Earl of Iveagh, shared his brother's vision.

Joseph Lister, 'father of antiseptic surgery'

The New Iveagh Trust flats at Kevin Street, near St James's Gate Brewery, c.1940–45

He was an extremely successful businessman and an untiring philanthropist. On his way to work from St Stephen's Green to the brewery, Edward Cecil witnessed terrible poverty. He could see the wretched living conditions of so many Dubliners, and he realised the importance of housing and medical care to the quality of their lives. He started on a programme to demolish the slums and build new homes in their place. Today, the Iveagh Trust in Dublin and The Guinness Trust in the UK carry on his good work, looking after tens of thousands of people.

When one of Edward Cecil's footmen was bitten by a rabid dog at his estate at Elveden in Suffolk in 1896, he made sure that his employee received the best available treatment. He was shocked to find that this meant sending him all the way to Paris to the Institut Pasteur. He determined that such treatment should be available in England and accordingly donated £5,000 to the newly formed British Institute of Preventive Medicine – later the Lister Institute of Preventive Medicine. Further support followed and the Lister Institute went on to achieve worldwide renown, being at the forefront of the fight against disease. Its targets ranged from smallpox, typhoid and diphtheria in the nineteenth century, to cancer, rheumatism and nutritional disorders in the twentieth century. This was thanks in part to a brewer from Dublin and his visionary philanthropy.

Promotional advertisement
for Guinness in Nigeria,
c.1960s

Guinness Overseas

PEOPLE HAVE BEEN ENJOYING Guinness beer in foreign climes for centuries. The earliest recorded export of stout from St James's Gate was in 1769, when it first made the trip to England. In 1801, Arthur Guinness I introduced a special brew for export, West India Porter (now known as Foreign Extra Stout), made with extra hops so that it could travel the high seas and still arrive in perfect condition.

Over the next thirty years, shipments were recorded to Lisbon, the southern states of America, the West Indies and sub-Saharan Africa. In 1858, almost 100 years after the brewery was founded, eighty cases, each containing three dozen bottles of Guinness, made their way to the southern hemisphere to be enjoyed in New Zealand. By 1870, one in ten bottles of the brew was being sold overseas.

The company had to rely on exporters to take the best care of its product, and concerns about quality lead to the opening of a number of overseas breweries. Guinness began by bottling

The map shows Guinness Draught is available in Europe, North America, South Africa, Australia, New Zealand and part of South East Asia, and Guinness Foreign Extra Stout in Africa, the Caribbean and Asia.

Guinness sales vans used for promotional activity in the USA, early 1960s

the product in local markets, and then started to brew the beer locally. The Park Royal brewery in London was opened in 1936, and the Ikeja brewery in Nigeria was opened in 1963 by my father, Benjamin Guinness, Chairman. He oversaw the expansion of the brew on an enormous scale, with the building of breweries in Malaysia (1965), Cameroon (1970), Ghana (1971) and Jamaica (1974).

Guinness is now brewed in over forty countries around the world and enjoyed in over 150 countries. And it can be found in the most inhospitable of places: legend has it that Australian adventurer Douglas Mawson made sure he packed a few bottles when he set out on his expedition to the South Pole in 1909. In each country, Guinness has taken on a slightly different personality. In Malaysia, a baby might be baptised with a little drop of the brew to give him strength, and I know that my wife Mira enjoys its nutritional qualities when nursing our children.

Official opening of the Cameroon Brewery, with Benjamin Guinness and the Cameroon Minister of Commerce and Industry toasting each other, 1970

Below: Ethiopia was the
51st country to brew
Guinness, 2001

Bottom: Transportation
of Guinness to the USA,
c.1960s

1930s press advert
recounting an Antarctic
expedition led by
Douglas Mawson

Alan Lennox Boyd,
family member and joint
Managing Director,
promoting Guinness
in Fiji, 1959

Below: Transportation
of Guinness in Malaysia,
c.1960s

Bottom: Sungei Way
Brewery, Malaysia,
opened 1965

This famous 1837 Phiz
illustration from Charles
Dickens's *Pickwick Papers*
shows a contemporary
advertisment for
Guinness stout

Guinness in Famous Hands

WHETHER AT HOME OR OVERSEAS, the great and the good have come together in praise of the inspirational qualities of Guinness beer. Arthur may only have taken possession of St James's Gate in 1759, but in 1797 Henry Grattan (1746–1821), who was a leading Irish Member of Parliament and a campaigner for legislative freedom for the Irish House of Commons, firmly declared that Irish beer was 'the nurse of the people and entitled to every encouragement and exemption'.

This precedent set, the first recorded reference to the export of Guinness followed in the same vein. An exhausted officer in Wellington's army at the Battle of Waterloo in 1815 made this entry in his diary the day after being wounded in battle:

'When I was sufficiently recovered to be permitted to take some nourishment, I felt the most extraordinary desire for a glass of Guinness, which I knew could be obtained without difficulty. Upon expressing my wish to the doctor, he told me I might take a small glass...It was not long before I sent for the

1933 press advert featuring a recommendation from a soldier who fought at the Battle of Waterloo

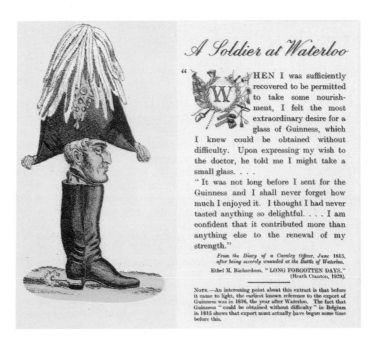

A Soldier at Waterloo

"WHEN I was sufficiently recovered to be permitted to take some nourishment, I felt the most extraordinary desire for a glass of Guinness, which I knew could be obtained without difficulty. Upon expressing my wish to the doctor, he told me I might take a small glass. . . .

"It was not long before I sent for the Guinness and I shall never forget how much I enjoyed it. I thought I had never tasted anything so delightful. . . . I am confident that it contributed more than anything else to the renewal of my strength."

From the Diary of a Cavalry Officer, June 1815, after being severely wounded at the Battle of Waterloo.

Ethel M. Richardson, " LONG FORGOTTEN DAYS." (Heath Cranton, 1928).

NOTE.—An interesting point about this extract is that before it came to light, the earliest known reference to the export of Guinness was in 1816, the year after Waterloo. The fact that Guinness " could be obtained without difficulty " in Belgium in 1815 shows that export must actually have begun some time before this.

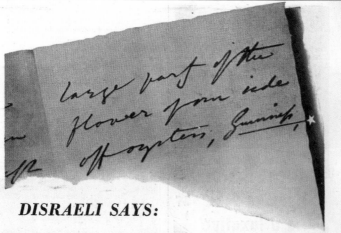

1930s press advert featuring a quotation by Benjamin Disraeli, 1837

DISRAELI SAYS:

"I supped at the Carlton— off Oysters and Guinness

thus ended the most remarkable day hitherto of my life"

The facsimile of an original letter from Disraeli to his sister Sarah, dated November 21, 1837. (In the collection of Mr. E. Thomas Cook.)

GUINNESS and oysters are just as much of a treat today as in Disraeli's time. Brewed in Dublin from barley malt, hops, yeast and water — and nothing else, Guinness has a dry hearty flavour which is the perfect accompaniment to oysters.

Guinness has been made by the same natural brewing process ever since 1759 and has become the most popular brew in the world. If you haven't yet tried Guinness and oysters, you're nearly two centuries behind the times.

Guinness is also enjoyed before meals, after exercise or when tired, and before retiring. You should be able to get it wherever you buy good beer or ale.

Since 1759

GUINNESS
IS GOOD FOR YOU

The story of Guinness since 1759: 108 pages, 52 illustrations. Write American Representative: A. Guinness, Son & Co., Ltd., Dept. 104-A, 501 Fifth Avenue, N. Y.

Copyright, 1937, by A. Guinness, Son & Co., Ltd. G. U. 104-C

Guinness and I shall never forget how much I enjoyed it. I thought I had never tasted anything so delightful... I am confident that it contributed more than anything else to the renewal of my strength.'

We also know that the British Prime Minister Benjamin Disraeli enjoyed the perfect combination of oysters and stout on the night of 21 November 1837, the day after he attended the meeting of the first parliament of Queen Victoria's reign – 'the most remarkable day hitherto of my life'. Disraeli later went on to become a friend of Benjamin Lee Guinness when he was an MP at the Westminster Parliament.

In 1861, London was brought to a standstill by the death of Albert, the Prince Consort of Queen Victoria. According to legend, the bar steward of Brooks' Club, an exclusive club for gentlemen in St James's, announced that even the champagne should be put into mourning – and added Guinness stout to the amber bubbly. This was not only respectful homage but it also gave birth to the magical Black Velvet cocktail.

Guinness beer has likewise been celebrated in literature. In 1837, Charles Dickens's *Pickwick Papers* showed Sam and Tony Weller with an advertisement for it in the background. James Joyce was introduced to Guinness by Oliver St John Gogarty and was so inspired by it that he included the brew in *Finnegan's Wake* and *Ulysses*.

It is known that Sean O'Casey enjoyed a pint, as did Brendan Behan and Patrick Kavanagh. And Oscar Wilde's father, Sir William Wilde, a pioneering oculist and antiquarian, was known to enjoy a glass with friends.

In February 1893, the novelist Robert Louis Stevenson, author of *Treasure Island*, wrote a letter from his cruise holiday. He cannot have been in the greatest form, since he was recovering from influenza. However, the nourishing thought of a glass of Guinness cheered him up: 'I shall be no sooner done with the present amanuensing racket than I shall put myself outside a pint of Guinness. If you think this looks like dying of consumption in Apia I can only say I differ from you.'

In James Joyce's Ulysses, *the Guinness brewery is cited in a long list of ancient treasures of Ireland.*

(Cyclops 12.1453–1454, Gabler edition)

Perhaps the most famous hands that Guinness ever found were through Norris and Ross McWhirter, the first editors of *The Guinness Book of Records*.

Sir Hugh Beavor was Managing Director of Guinness in 1951, when he missed some golden plover whilst out shooting in Co. Wexford in Ireland. There ensued a great discussion about what was the fastest game bird, but no one knew the answer. This gave him the idea of publishing an authoritative fact book to end all pub debates.

His colleague at the brewery was Chris Chataway, the famous athlete. Chataway knew of the twins at Oxford University – the McWhirters – who ran a fact-finding agency. The introduction was to pave the way to an outstanding publishing success story.

James Joyce submitted a slogan to the brewery once: 'The free, the flow, the frothy freshener'.

However, this got passed over for the snappier if less alliterative 'Guinness is good for you'.

A LETTER FROM
Robert Louis Stevenson

"... *Fanny ate a whole fowl for breakfast, to say nothing of a tower of hot cakes. Belle and I floored another hen betwixt the pair of us, and I shall be no sooner done with the present amanuensing racket than I shall put myself outside a pint of Guinness. If you think this looks like dying of consumption in the South Seas I can only say I differ from you.*"

This was written by Robert Louis Stevenson from Samoa, to Sidney Colvin in London, on February 19th, 1893.

We know the happy effect the climate of Samoa had on the health of Robert Louis Stevenson, and what English literature owes to the South Seas. But we did not know until we read this letter that Stevenson had Guinness there. When we think of the transportation problems in that part of the world in the 1890's, not to mention expense, his compliment to Guinness seems all the more remarkable.

It may interest you to hear that the Guinness sold at your corner shop today is the same Guinness which Stevenson mentions. Made the same way, of the same materials, aged just as long.

And if you would like to know how Stevenson felt after he got outside that pint, you have only to follow his example.

GUINNESS
IS GOOD FOR YOU

The story of Guinness since 1759: 108 pages, 52 illustrations. Write American Representative: A. Guinness, Son & Co., Ltd., Dept. 70A, 501 Fifth Avenue, New York   GU-700

Guinness Advertising

NO OTHER PRODUCT in the history of advertising has been sold more imaginatively, or has enjoyed such an affectionate relationship with the public. You would not have thought it, but Guinness was quite late onto the advertising scene in the 1920s. Other well-known companies had been advertising for more than twenty years when Lord Iveagh decided that it was time for a campaign. If Guinness had to advertise, he announced, it must advertise well.

The Guinness board appointed S. H. Benson Ltd, one of the leading advertising agencies of its day, and gave its Director Oswald Greene the job of finding the right message for Guinness's first campaign. Greene began by visiting the Guinness brewery in Dublin, where he studied every aspect of

Gilroy's famous ostrich poster, 1936, in which the bird is shown having swallowed the glass the 'wrong way up'

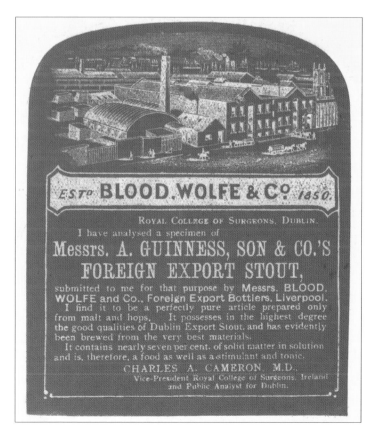

Label for Guinness stout, bottled by Blood, Wolfe and Co., c.1880

the beer's production. Not satisfied with the results of this visit, he went on an extended pub crawl with his colleague Bobby Bevan. The two men visited a great number of pubs in Dublin, and in each one they asked the Guinness drinkers why they drank it. Amazingly, the answer was usually the same: 'We drink it because it's good for us!'

Greene and Bevan realised that they did not need to look any further for a slogan, and in 1929 the first UK press advertisement appeared, stating for the very first time that 'Guinness is Good for You'. Having made such a bold claim, Lord Iveagh wanted to back it up. Why exactly was Guinness good for you? Further advertisements informed the public that it was good for strength, nerves, digestion, exhaustion and sleeplessness. Doctors already prescribed Guinness beer for nursing mothers and convalescents, and the advertising message received strong support from the medical profession. Charles A. Cameron, Vice-President of the Royal College of Surgeons, Dublin, stated in an advertisement that the drink was 'a food as well as a stimulant and tonic.'

The Guinness Animals

Who would use a load of naughty animals to sell beer? The madness started with John Gilroy, a creative genius working at Benson's advertising agency. When Gilroy was visiting Bertram Mills' Circus at Olympia he saw a sea lion skilfully balancing objects on its nose. He

My GOODNESS –
My GUINNESS

Kangaroo poster, 1947

then imagined that one of these objects might be a pint of Guinness. 'My Goodness!' the audience would have gasped, and so Gilroy began to make the link with the Goodness of Guinness. The animals, with their unique characters, inspired Gilroy to create an entire family of misbehaving creatures, as well as the poor zoo keeper, forever chasing those escaping glasses of Guinness.

Sea lion poster, 1935

Lion poster, 1937

If he can say as you can

"Guinness is good for you"

How grand to be a Toucan-

Just think what Toucan do!

Dorothy L. Sayers wrote the copy for this first toucan poster, 1935

The Guinness toucan started life as a pelican on Gilroy's drawing board, but when Dorothy L. Sayers was asked to find some suitable copy for the pelican, she realised that a toucan offered much better possibilities. 'If he can say as you can, "Guinness is good for you", How grand to be a Toucan, Just think what Toucan do'. The toucan became much plumper over the years, and its beak grew much shorter. However, the plastic surgeons were sure to keep his beak long enough to accommodate at least a couple of pints of Guinness.

From 1935 until the present day, these wonderful animals have delighted successive generations. They appeared on the

Bear poster, 1956

My Goodness — My GUINNESS

My GOODNESS –
My GUINNESS

Pelican poster, 1939

RAF toucan poster, 1955

sides of buses and on advertising hoardings throughout the UK and Ireland. In 1979, the toucan made it onto the television. 'Help! He's Toucan Off – Big Flap as Bird in Advert Escapes!' read one headline the following day.

You might notice that in the ostrich poster (see page 52), the bird has swallowed the glass the wrong way up. There was a torrent of mail to the brewery from anxious customers

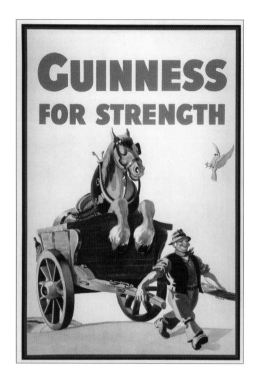

pointing this out. However, the artist had realised that if the glass was shown the correct way around (that is, upside down), then it looked surprisingly like a weight from a set of scales. Not quite what the artist ordered! Of course, such a prosaic answer would never do. Gilroy informed the public that the ostrich had been imitating the sea lion by balancing the glass on its nose; it had then flicked the glass up into the air and opened its beak. Thankfully the ostrich could still enjoy his Guinness, hence his cheeky, satisfied grin.

The toucan (1935), the sea lion (1935), the tortoise (1936), the ostrich (1936) and the zoo keeper (1937) were the most famous of characters. Others that didn't make the cut included a bull, a beaver, a donkey, a cobra, an elephant and a woodpecker. All of these animals had strong associations with other brands, or sports, or were just too scary!

And so the Guinness animals started a whole genre of advertising which has been adored ever since.

Guinness For Strength
poster, 1949

Guinness For Strength
poster, 1934

Overleaf:
Dripmats, 1950s–2000s

Guinness Him Strong!
poster, 1961

Poster commemorating
900 years since the Battle
of Hastings

Poster issued in Ireland
as part of an advertising
campaign called
'Pure Magic'

First published in 2009 by
Scala Publishers Ltd
Northburgh House
10 Northburgh Street
London EC1V 0AT

www.scalapublishers.com

ISBN: 978 1 85759 582 6

Project Editor: Sandra Pisano
Designer: Nigel Soper
Printed in Spain

10 9 8 7 6 5 4 3 2 1

Photographic credits

All images courtesy of
Guinness Archive,
Diageo Ireland and Guinness
Storehouse, except:
Illustrations (pp. 8, 16, 26, 27,
50): Jeremy Williams.
Photograph of Joseph Lister
(page 36): Reproduced by kind
permission of The Royal
Veterinary College.
'Storm before the Calm' poster
(page 61): Courtesy of Irish
International BBDO.
'Smiling G' dripmat (page 62):
© Estate of Abram Games.
Gilroy Animals (back flap):
Courtesy of Miranda Iveagh.

Picture research:
Mira Guinness

Inside front cover: Guinness
float for St Patrick's Day
Parade, Limerick, 1960.
Inside back cover: One of the
world-famous Guinness gates,
St James's Gate Brewery.